Ann
Secι

GW01417447

Written by Barrie Wade and Maggie Moore
Illustrated by Bethan Matthews

Collins Educational
An Imprint of HarperCollinsPublishers

Anna and Kim were in the playground. It was nearly time for school to start.

"I've got a secret," said Anna importantly.

"What is it," said Kim.

"Oh, I can't tell you. It's a secret," replied Anna.

"Then don't talk about it," said Kim.

The bell went and the two girls walked
in together.

In the cloakroom Anna said, "It's a very
special secret."

Kim said, "Well, I'm your special friend. So
tell me."

"Can't," said Anna, and she walked away.

In the classroom Miss Scott was busy taking the register.

"Get on with your topic work, everyone," she said. "You know what to do."

The children stopped talking, got out their books and started to work. Miss Scott watched them over the top of her glasses and then went back to marking the register.

Kim prodded Anna with a pencil and passed her a note. It said:

You can tell me the secret because we are in a secret club.

Anna read the note. She looked at Miss Scott who was still busy and then she wrote a note back to Kim. Anna gave it to Kim and got on with her work. Kim opened the note. It said:

I can't tell this secret.

At playtime Anna and Kim went outside together. Kim wanted to play some clapping games but Anna danced around saying, "I've got a secret, I've got a secret."

Kim asked again, "What is it?"

Anna ran off shouting, "Can't tell, can't tell."

Kim felt cross and upset. She and Anna were good friends. They usually told each other everything. She didn't like the way her friend was teasing her.

Pete and Kulbir were playing hopscotch in the playground. They saw Anna run off and leave Kim behind.

"What's wrong with Anna?" asked Pete.

Kim answered, "She keeps saying she's got a secret and can't tell me what it is."

Pete said, "It wouldn't be a secret if she told you."

"I know that," said Kim, "but she keeps on teasing and it makes me cross."

Kulbir said, "Oh, forget it. Come and play with us."

The three of them played football until playtime was over, and Kim felt better.

On their way back to the classroom, Pete whispered to Anna, "Hey, Anna, what's your secret?"

"I'm not telling," said Anna. "It's special."

"Go on," said Pete. "We're in a secret club. We can share secrets."

"No," said Anna.

"Oh, all right then," said Pete, "I don't want to know."

Kulbir said, "I don't either."

Kim said, "I don't either."

Anna looked very surprised.

The next lesson was art. Pete, Kulbir, Anna and Kim sat in a group as usual. Today they had to draw a pair of old, dirty shoes and an apple. Miss Scott said it was 'Still Life'.

"I wouldn't like to eat an apple after it's been near those shoes," said Pete to Kim.

"No, especially if the tongue had licked it," Kim said quickly. Nobody else got the joke.

Anna stopped drawing and wrote another note to Kim.

My secret is very special.

Kim wrote back. Her note said:

I don't want to know. I'm not your friend any more.

She pushed her note across the table.

At dinnertime Kim sat near Sally to eat her lunch. There was no room for Anna. Then Kim played football with Sally. They didn't ask Anna to join in. Anna stood and watched.

"What's wrong now?" asked Pete.

"Kim says she's not my friend," said Anna.

Kulbir groaned, "Oh, no. You two are always falling out."

Anna said crossly, "Oh, no we aren't."

Pete laughed and said, "You just have."

That afternoon, Anna took no notice of Kim. She laughed and giggled with Emma. She got into trouble with Miss Scott for being so noisy.

Kim got into trouble, too. She was telling jokes to Sally and made mistakes in her work. She had to do it again.

Kim and Anna didn't walk home together, like they always did before.

When Kim got home she was in tears.

Kim's Dad was at home working on the computer. He asked her what was wrong.

Kim said, "I've fallen out with Anna. She wouldn't tell me her secret."

Mr Luk said, "That's a silly reason for falling out. Some secrets aren't meant to be told."

18

"I know," said Kim, still sniffling.

"So what are you going to do about it?" asked her Dad.

"I'll write her a note, with a joke in it," said Kim.

"Good idea," said her Dad.

When Anna got home she was in tears.

Anna's mum asked her what was wrong. Anna said, "I've fallen out with Kim because I wouldn't tell her the secret."

Anna's mum said, "But it isn't a secret. You can tell Kim when you like."

Anna was still sniffling a little. "I really wanted to tell Kim but I also wanted to keep my secret to myself," she said. "I'll tell her tomorrow and we'll be friends again."

"I've got a better idea," said her mum, and she told Anna her plan.

The next day Kim walked up to Anna in the playground and gave her a note.

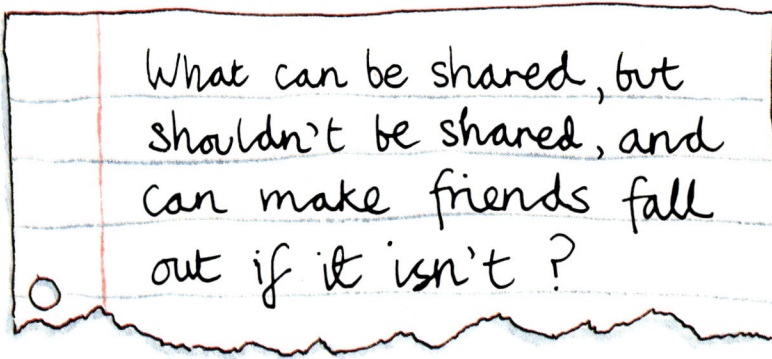

> What can be shared, but shouldn't be shared, and can make friends fall out if it isn't?

Anna said, "I know the answer to that. *A secret.* I'm going to tell you my secret today, but can you wait until after school?"

Kim told Anna she *would* wait to hear the secret. The two girls went into school together, giggling happily.

Kulbir looked at them. "Kim and Anna are friends again," he said.

"I knew they would be," said Pete, and he ran into school with Kulbir.

At hometime, Anna asked Kim to wait with her until her mum came.

"There's my mum now," said Anna, waving her hand.

Kim could see that
Anna's mum was
holding something
under her coat.
Kim saw two soft,
golden ears, two
sleepy, blue eyes and
a damp little nose.

Anna said happily, "That's my secret."

"Oh," said Kim. "What a lovely kitten. What
are you going to call her?"

"Koppi," said Anna.

"Koppi?" asked Kim, looking puzzled.

"Yes," said Anna. "Koppi Cat."